Kingdom Carriers

Living, Leading, and Loving on Mission in the End Times
By Jacob Isaac

I0159711

Copyright

Chapter 1

Wake Up, Warrior!

"... it is high time to awake out of sleep; for now our salvation is nearer than when we first believed."

—Romans 13:11 (NKJV)

The Alarm Is Sounding

This is not just another book. This is not just another devotional.

This is an alarm clock.

Because the hour is later than we think.

We live in a world sedated by entertainment, distracted by comfort, and lulled to sleep by a false sense of normal. But Heaven is not quiet. The Spirit is not passive. And God is not pacing the floor in worry—He's calling. Loudly. Boldly. Urgently.

He's calling you.

Not to fear—but to wake up.

Not to hide—but to stand up.

Not to survive—but to carry the Kingdom.

Born for This Hour

You could have been born in any generation. But God placed you here—in this moment, in this hour, in this battlefield of culture, confusion, and compromise—for a reason.

Esther was told, "You were born for such a time as this." So were you.

You are not late to the party. You are right on time for the mission.

You're not too old.

You're not too young.

You're not too broken.

You're not too far behind.

God doesn't call the polished—He commissions the willing.

And if you've ever felt that holy restlessness... if you've ever sensed that something in your spirit won't sit still... if you've looked at the world and whispered, "Surely there must be more"—you're hearing the call.

You're one of His Kingdom Carriers.

Christianity was Never Meant to be Comfortable

We've built stages when we were meant to build altars.

We've followed influencers instead of following Jesus.

We've played it safe while souls are slipping away.

But real Kingdom Carriers don't blend in. They burn.

They're the ones who show up early to pray and stay late to serve.

They're the quiet ones sowing faithfully where no one sees.

They're the ones with spiritual fire in their belly, even if the world calls them strange.

The days of lukewarm faith must end. The stakes are too high.

It's time to wake up.

When God is Looking for a Voice, Will He Find You?

There's a story in the Bible where the Lord searches for someone to stand in the gap, to be a voice, to carry His heart to a broken people. He says:

"I looked for someone among them who would build up the wall and stand before me in the gap on behalf of the land..."

—Ezekiel 22:30 (NIV)

But no one answered.

Let that not be said of us.

When God is looking for a voice in this generation, may He find you.

When He's looking for someone to weep with the broken and war in prayer, may He find you.

When He's searching for a messenger who won't dilute the message, may He find you.

You may not feel ready. But if you're willing, He will empower you.

There's No Neutral in the Spirit

Make no mistake: in this hour, passivity is participation. Silence is agreement. Indifference is surrender.

You're either pushing back darkness—or tolerating it.

You're either advancing the Kingdom—or retreating in fear.

You're either carrying the flame—or watching it flicker out.

And let's be clear—carrying the Kingdom doesn't mean being loud and angry online. It means being faithful in prayer, bold in obedience, and humble in spirit.

It's the mum raising Kingdom kids when no one is cheering.

It's the worker praying over spreadsheets and cubicles.

It's the intercessor waking in the night to pray for nations they've never stepped foot in.

These are Kingdom Carriers. And they are not asleep.

A Sleeping Church Cannot Wake a Dying World

If we're spiritually asleep, how can we sound the alarm for others?

We need more than inspirational quotes and emotional highs.

We need revival—not the tent kind, but the heart kind.

A deep return to Jesus. A fierce loyalty to His voice. A bold surrender to His will.

The early Church didn't have microphones, money, or marketing. But they had fire. And the world could not stop them.

If you've been tired, distracted, or stuck in spiritual fog, let this be your wake-up moment.

Shake off the dust. Wipe the slumber from your eyes. You were made for more.

God is Not Looking for the Next Celebrity — He's Looking for the Next Carrier

You don't need a platform.

You don't need perfect words.

You don't need a theological degree.

You need a **willing heart**.

A heart that says, "Here I am, Lord. Send me."

A heart that breaks for what breaks His.

A heart that listens when others walk away.

A heart that lives with the end in mind—and eternity in focus.

The world doesn't need more polished preachers.

It needs **burning ones.**

The ones who carry the Kingdom.

Not just in sermons—but in silence.

Not just on Sundays—but on street corners and staff meetings and supermarkets and slums.

You are that carrier.

Final Charge: Wake Up and Carry the Flame

If you hear anything in this book, let it be this:

You don't need a title to be a terror to hell.

You don't need permission to say yes to Jesus.

You don't need a crowd to change the course of history.

You just need to wake up, warrior!

Because the King is coming.

The harvest is ready.

And the hour is now.

Prayer

Father, wake me up from any place of apathy or fear.

Let my heart burn again with holy urgency.

Give me eyes to see, ears to hear, and feet that move at Your whisper.

I don't want to sleep through the season You've placed me in.

Make me alert, bold, and available.

I surrender my comfort for Your commission.

In Jesus' name, amen.

Reflection Questions

1. Where have I settled into spiritual comfort or autopilot?

2. What signs of the times am I noticing around me, and how is God calling me to respond?

3. In what specific ways can I begin carrying the Kingdom in my current sphere of influence?

Kingdom Declaration

I am not asleep.

I am not afraid.

I am a Kingdom Carrier.

I carry His fire, His love, and His truth.

I was born for this hour.

I will not back down.

I will wake up, stand up, and speak up—until He returns.

Chapter 2

What Is a Kingdom Carrier?

"As the Father has sent Me, I also send you."
—John 20:21 (NKJV)

Not a Title—a Mandate

You don't need a ministry title to make Kingdom impact.

You don't need to be behind a pulpit to carry spiritual authority.

You don't need thousands of followers to move heaven and shake earth.

A Kingdom Carrier is not defined by status, fame, or platform.

A Kingdom Carrier is defined by surrender.

It's someone who says "yes" when others hesitate.

Someone who carries the Presence of God into forgotten places, unglamorous spaces, and hard conversations.

Someone who lives sent—whether across the globe or across the street.

Carrying the Kingdom Means Carrying the King

To be a Kingdom Carrier is to be a **Presence Carrier.**

You're not just carrying ideas about God—you're carrying **God Himself.** His love. His power. His voice. His values. His mission.

Where you walk, **He walks.**

Where you speak, **He echoes.**

When you pray, **He responds.**

You don't represent yourself. You represent Heaven.

It's not about how impressive you are—it's about how present He is.

This is not religious hype. This is spiritual reality.

You are a walking, talking, surrendered vessel of the living King.

God Uses Ordinary People Who Say "Yes"

Throughout Scripture, God used people who didn't look qualified:

A stuttering shepherd to speak before Pharaoh (Moses)

A young boy to slay a giant (David)

A former prostitute to shelter spies (Rahab)

A fisherman to lead the early church (Peter)

A persecutor to become an apostle (Paul)

Why?

Because God's not after credentials—He's after availability.

You might feel ordinary. But God does **extraordinary things** with ordinary people who carry Him.

From Sunday Christians to Everyday Carriers

Many people treat Christianity like an event—something to attend, consume, or check off on a Sunday.

But Kingdom Carriers aren't weekend warriors. They're **everyday missionaries.**

That means you don't leave Jesus in the church foyer.

You bring Him into meetings, coffee catchups, classrooms, hospitals, prisons, and politics.

Kingdom Carriers don't compartmentalise faith. They **integrate it.**

The Kingdom doesn't clock out.

The Kingdom doesn't wait for permission.

The Kingdom is not stuck inside four walls.

And neither are you.

Assignment Over Applause

Let's be honest—the temptation to impress is real.

We live in a culture obsessed with influence, applause, and platform-building. But God is raising a different kind of leader—one who cares more about **obedience** than attention.

Kingdom Carriers are faithful even when it's not popular.

They show up even when there's no spotlight.

They obey even when it's hard.

You don't carry the Kingdom to be seen—you carry it because the King is worthy.

You are not on a popularity contest.

You are on assignment.

The Weight and Wonder of Carrying the Kingdom

This is not a light thing.

To carry the Kingdom means you walk in spiritual authority—but also spiritual responsibility.

You are a steward of divine influence.

You are a vessel of reconciliation.

You are a light in dark places.

This isn't something you put on like a costume.

It's something you **become.**

You carry truth that confronts lies.

You carry mercy that disrupts judgement.

You carry justice that refuses to be silent.

And yes—it will cost you.

But oh, it's worth it.

The World Needs What You Carry

Someone's breakthrough is on the other side of your obedience.

Someone's healing is connected to your "yes".

Someone's hope is tied to your voice, your prayer, your hands.

You carry peace in places of panic.

You carry purpose in spaces of confusion.

You carry the King in places others have abandoned.

That's why the enemy tries so hard to convince you that you're too broken, too busy, too late, or too ordinary.

Because if you ever **fully believe who you are in Christ...**

If you ever realise what you actually carry...

If you ever walk into a room knowing Heaven walks in with you...

Darkness won't stand a chance.

Prayer

King Jesus, thank You for trusting me to carry Your Kingdom. I confess where I've disqualified myself or believed the lie that I'm not enough. Today, I say "yes" again to Your call. Use me wherever You want—in public or private, with platform or without. Let Your Presence be evident in how I live, speak, serve, and love. I carry You not in arrogance, but in awe. Empower me to represent You well. In Jesus' name, amen.

Reflection Questions

1. Where have I believed the lie that I'm not qualified to carry the Kingdom?

2. How can I be more intentional about living as a Kingdom Carrier in everyday spaces?

3. What might God be asking me to carry into my current sphere of influence?

Kingdom Declaration

I am a Kingdom Carrier.

I carry His Presence, His power, and His purpose.

I am not waiting for a platform—I am living on assignment.

I am not defined by titles—I am defined by surrender.

I say "yes" to the call.

I walk with the King.

And I carry the Kingdom—wherever I go.

Chapter 3

Living on Mission, Not on Autopilot

"Go therefore and make disciples of all the nations..."
—Matthew 28:19 (NKJV)

You Are Already Sent

Mission isn't for a select few who board planes to distant lands.

Mission is for you—right where you are.

If you follow Jesus, you're not waiting to be sent; **you are already sent**.

The question isn't "Am I called?" but "Am I willing?"

Being a Kingdom Carrier means refusing to coast through life like a passenger. It means living with a **sense of divine assignment**—every day, everywhere.

Life is Too Short for Autopilot

Autopilot is convenient when flying a plane, but it's deadly for your spiritual life.

Autopilot faith says, "Just get through the week."

Autopilot faith drifts, blends in, and avoids risk.

Autopilot faith ignores the whisper of the Spirit.

But mission-minded believers wake up every morning with a sense of purpose:

"Lord, how can I carry Your Kingdom today?"

Mission Is Identity, Not Geography

You are a missionary—not because you crossed an ocean, but because Jesus crossed eternity for you.

A teacher shaping the next generation is a missionary.

A parent praying over children at night is a missionary.

A business owner leading with integrity is a missionary.

A young person choosing holiness in a world of compromise is a missionary.

Wherever you are—**that's your mission field.**

Stop Waiting for Perfect Conditions

We often delay obedience, thinking, "When I'm ready... when I know more... when I have more resources..."

But Kingdom Carriers don't wait for all the lights to turn green. They move when the King says move.

Jesus didn't wait until His disciples had it all figured out. He sent them while they were still learning.

Why? Because obedience **creates growth.**

Don't wait to feel perfect. Start where you are, with what you have. Heaven will back you up.

Ordinary Moments Become Holy Ground

The mission of God is not just found in big stages or dramatic stories.

It's found in the **ordinary moments:**

A quiet word of encouragement to a weary co-worker.

A prayer whispered in a hospital waiting room.

A meal shared with someone the world overlooks.

A generous act that no one sees but God.

When your heart is surrendered, even the smallest actions carry eternal weight.

Mission Requires Margin

We can't live on mission if we're constantly overbooked, overwhelmed, and overextended.

Mission thrives in margin—in the spaces where we slow down, listen to the Spirit, and notice people.

Jesus often paused for the one—the blind man calling out, the woman at the well, the tax collector in a tree.

Being on mission means living **interruptible**—open to divine appointments.

Carrying Hope Where It Hurts Most

Everywhere you go, you're surrounded by silent battles.

People wear smiles while carrying pain.

They're longing for someone to notice, to listen, to bring hope.

That's what Kingdom Carriers do.

We don't just see problems—we see **people.**

We don't just talk about light—we **bring** light.

The workplace, the café, the bus stop, the school gate—these are all pulpits, if you're willing.

Faith in Motion

The Great Commission was never a suggestion. It's the heartbeat of Heaven.

Jesus didn't say, "Sit and wait." He said, "Go and make."

Mission isn't about striving harder; it's about aligning your life with the King's agenda.

If you feel stuck or stagnant, maybe it's because you've been living in observation mode.

It's time to shift into **participation mode.**

Mission begins where you are.

It flows through who you are.

And it points to Who He is.

Prayer

Lord, I don't want to drift through life on autopilot. Wake me up to the mission You've placed before me. Help me see my workplace, my neighbourhood, and my everyday spaces as part of Your Kingdom plan. Give me boldness to speak when needed, compassion to act when prompted, and wisdom to love like You. I choose to live sent—today and every day. In Jesus' name, amen.

Reflection Questions

1. What areas of my life have I placed on "autopilot", ignoring God's mission?

2. Who in my current circle needs to experience the love of Christ through me this week?

3. What practical step can I take to live with greater Kingdom intentionality?

Kingdom Declaration

I am on mission.

I refuse to live on autopilot.

I carry the presence and power of God into every space I enter.

I am sent—right here, right now.

I will live with purpose, passion, and faith—until the King returns.

Chapter 4

Discerning the Times Without Losing Your Mind

"...understanding the present time: The hour has already come for you to wake up from your slumber..."

—Romans 13:11 (NIV)

The Noise Is Deafening

Wars. Earthquakes. Political upheaval. Global pandemics.

Social media chaos. Division. Fear. Hatred. Confusion.

The headlines are heavy, the world is shaking, and everywhere you turn, people are asking:

"What in the world is going on?"

But while culture panics and darkness spreads, Kingdom Carriers don't lose their minds.

They **discern the times**—and they **anchor their hearts.**

We are not called to be **overwhelmed by the shaking.**

We are called to be **unshaken in the storm.**

We Are in the Last Days

This is not conspiracy—it's prophecy.

Jesus told us the signs to look for:

Nation rising against nation

Lawlessness increasing

Love growing cold

Good being called evil, and evil being called good

Sound familiar?

The earth isn't just groaning—**it's screaming**.

But the shaking is not meant to make us fear.

It's meant to make us **ready.**

Discernment Over Distraction

The enemy doesn't need to destroy you if he can distract you.

14

And let's be honest—many believers are so glued to their phones that they've stopped listening to Heaven.

We scroll for hours and pray for minutes.

We react to culture but neglect to sit with the Word.

We argue about politics but stay silent in the place of prayer.

Kingdom Carriers are called to live differently.

We're not driven by breaking news—we're grounded by **unbreaking truth.**

We don't parrot everything we hear—we test it in the Spirit.

We don't follow every trend—we follow the voice of the King.

Don't Confuse Information with Revelation

Having access to information doesn't mean you have insight.

Google can give you facts—but only the Holy Spirit gives **discernment.**

Discerning the times doesn't mean becoming paranoid or suspicious.

It means walking with wisdom, prayer, and spiritual sensitivity.

You may not understand every headline, but you can **understand the season.**

And more importantly, you can understand your role in it.

Stay Awake, Not Anxious

It's possible to be **alert** without being **afraid.**

To be **awake** without being **angry.**

To be **engaged** without being **consumed.**

Philippians 4:7 says: "The peace of God, which surpasses all understanding, will guard your hearts and minds through Christ Jesus."

That means even in global chaos—**you can have peace.**

Not because things are easy, but because your roots run deep.

Not because you understand everything, but because you trust the One who does.

Anchored in Truth, Not Trends

When the world is shaking, people will look for something stable.

Let them find you—**unmoved, unafraid**, and **anchored.**

How?

Stay in the Word daily

Guard your thought life

Stay in community with other believers

Ask the Holy Spirit for discernment before reacting

Fast when you feel spiritually dull

Keep eternity in focus

Kingdom Carriers aren't trend chasers.

They're truth walkers.

Be a Watchman, Not a Worrier

In the Bible, God raised up **watchmen**—people who would stay alert, sound the alarm, and pray with purpose.

That's your role.

You don't carry the weight of the world—but you carry the heart of Heaven.

You don't need to solve everything—but you need to **stand in the gap.**

When others are panicking, you'll be **interceding.**

When others are ranting, you'll be **worshipping.**

When others are giving up, you'll be **pressing in.**

This is what Kingdom Carriers do.

Prayer

Holy Spirit, teach me to discern the times. Help me not to be distracted, anxious, or overwhelmed. Anchor me in truth. Give me a clear mind and a steady heart. Show me how to live with urgency but not fear—with boldness, not burnout. I choose to trust You above every report, every headline, and every shaking. Use me as a watchman, a voice, and a vessel of peace in the chaos. In Jesus' name, amen.

Reflection Questions

1. Where have I allowed fear, news, or distractions to cloud my spiritual discernment?

2. What's one practical way I can stay spiritually anchored in this season?

3. Who around me is anxious or overwhelmed—and how can I carry peace to them?

Kingdom Declaration

I will not be shaken.

I will not be deceived.

I walk with wisdom, discernment, and peace.

I see the signs of the times—and I rise with holy urgency.

I am a watchman.

I am a Kingdom Carrier.

And I will not lose my mind—I will use it for the glory of God.

Chapter 5

Partnering with the Underground Church

"Remember the prisoners as if chained with them—those who are mistreated—since you yourselves are in the body also."

—Hebrews 13:3 (NKJV)

There Is a Church That Doesn't Meet on Sundays

They gather in secret.

They whisper their worship.

They hide their Bibles beneath floorboards.

They pray in code and preach in hushed tones.

They are **the underground church.**

While much of the Western church debates comfort, branding, and convenience, there are believers around the world who are risking their lives just to own a Bible—let alone read one.

And yet, they are not weak.

They are not struggling.

They are **revival fire.**

They Don't Need Our Pity—They Need Our Partnership

The underground church doesn't want sympathy.

They want **intercession.**

They want **courageous brothers and sisters.**

They want us to remember we're part of the same Body.

They don't need our slick sermons or social media strategies.

They need us to weep with them.

To pray like them.

To learn from them.

They may be hidden from the public eye, but they are **seen in Heaven.**

Faith That Costs Something

In persecuted nations, following Jesus can mean:

Losing your job
Being disowned by family
Imprisonment
Beatings
Even death

And yet—they **still follow.**
Still preach.
Still sing.
Still gather.
Still carry the Kingdom.
Their faith is not casual—it's costly.
But in that cost, there's glory.
Because Jesus is worth everything.

They Are Not Just Survivors—They Are Soldiers

The underground church is not just barely hanging on.

They are leading in miracles, discipleship, and endurance.

They are planting churches faster than the government can shut them down.

They are baptising by candlelight in bathtubs and rivers.

They don't just pray for comfort—they pray for boldness.

They don't ask for escape—they ask for empowerment.

And they don't shrink back. They rise up.

What Does Partnership Look Like?

To partner with the underground church doesn't mean rescuing them—it means **joining them.**

Here's how:

Pray regularly for the persecuted Church by name and nation.

Give strategically to missions and ministries that serve unreached and restricted areas.

Speak wisely—don't expose names or locations that could endanger lives.

Learn humbly—read their testimonies, honour their endurance, and model their grit.

Live boldly—let their courage stir yours.

Partnership starts with awareness but must move to **action.**

The Global Body is One

If one part of the Body suffers, all suffer.

If one part rejoices, all rejoice.

There is no Western Church and Underground Church in Heaven. There is just **the Church**—One Body, One Bride.

You may never meet these believers until eternity.

But your prayers matter.

Your giving matters.

Your example matters.

Because when you strengthen your part of the Body—**they feel it.**

Don't Wait Until it Comes to Your Door

Persecution may feel far off now—but make no mistake, the pressure is rising.

Bold preaching is already called hate speech.

Biblical values are already mocked.

Truth is already censored.

The underground church is not behind us—they are **ahead of us.**

And perhaps we're not the mature ones in the global church.

Perhaps they are.

Perhaps we need to **follow their example** instead of assuming they need to catch up to ours.

Prayer

Father, thank You for the faithful brothers and sisters who follow You under threat, danger, and persecution. Strengthen them. Provide for them. Protect them. And use me—in prayer, in giving, in living—to stand with them. Let me not be numb or distracted while they are kneeling and pressing in. Teach me to carry the Kingdom with the same courage, humility, and urgency. In Jesus' name, amen.

Reflection Questions

1. How often do I pray for or even think about the persecuted church?

2. In what ways has my faith become too comfortable or convenient?

3. What practical steps can I take to partner with or support the underground church?

Kingdom Declaration

I stand with my persecuted brothers and sisters.

I will not live a soft faith in a world that needs bold carriers.

I will pray with urgency.

I will give with strategy.

I will live with courage.

We are one Body. One Kingdom. One Church.

And I will carry the Kingdom—even in the shadows.

Chapter 6
Keys to Kingdom Obedience

"To obey is better than sacrifice, and to heed is better than the fat of rams."

—1 Samuel 15:22 (NIV)

Obedience Is Not Optional

In the Kingdom, obedience is not a suggestion. It's the starting point.

It's not just about what we believe—it's about **what we do** with what we believe.

Obedience isn't about rules—it's about **relationship**.

It's about trusting the King so deeply that when He speaks, you move.

Jesus never said, "Well done, good and successful servant."

He said, "Well done, good and faithful servant."

Faithfulness looks like obedience—in public and in private.

Delayed Obedience is Disobedience

We often tell God "yes," but then follow up with "later".

But in the Kingdom, **delayed obedience is still disobedience.**

Every time we postpone the nudge of the Holy Spirit, we're choosing comfort over calling.

Convenience over conviction.

Safety over surrender.

God doesn't bless hesitation—He honours **movement.**

If He said go, go.

If He said forgive, forgive.

If He said speak, speak.

Partial obedience is still rebellion in disguise.

Obedience Doesn't Always Make Sense—But It Always Bears Fruit

Noah built an ark in the middle of a drought.

Abraham prepared to sacrifice his promised son.

Peter stepped out of a boat onto water.

None of these made logical sense. But all were acts of **radical obedience.**

And because of that obedience, generations were changed.

Kingdom Carriers walk by faith, not by formulas.

We don't always need to understand the why—we just need to trust the **Who.**

Private Obedience Prepares You for Public Impact

Everyone wants the platform, but few are willing to say yes in the secret place.

Before David ever faced Goliath publicly, he obeyed God privately—slaying lions and bears in the field when no one was watching.

Your most powerful Kingdom assignments will be birthed in hidden places:

When you forgive without applause

When you intercede in silence

When you give sacrificially without being seen

Private obedience is Heaven's training ground.

Obedience Over Outcomes

God doesn't measure your obedience by how successful it looks—but by how surrendered your heart is.

You might obey and still get misunderstood.

You might obey and still face hardship.

You might obey and not see the fruit immediately.

But results are not your responsibility—**obedience is.**

Leave the outcomes to God.

The Enemy Fears Your Obedience

The devil isn't afraid of your Christian t-shirt or your highlight reel.

He's terrified of your **yes** to God.

Because one act of obedience can:

Break generational chains

Release revival

Shift entire communities

Unlock miracles

Silence darkness

Obedience shakes hell.

That's why the enemy distracts you, delays you, and discourages you. He knows your **yes** carries weight.

Costly Obedience, Eternal Reward

True obedience will cost you something:

Your pride

Your convenience

Your comfort

Your control

Maybe even your reputation

But what you gain is infinitely greater:

God's presence

God's favour

God's backing

God's reward

Jesus obeyed all the way to the Cross. And because of that obedience, salvation was made available to the world.

The Kingdom advances through people who obey—even when it's hard.

Prayer

Father, I surrender again. Forgive me for where I've delayed or resisted Your voice. Make me sensitive to Your whisper and bold in my response. I want to obey quickly, fully, and joyfully. Not because I have to—but because I love You. Let my obedience carry weight in Heaven. In Jesus' name, amen.

Reflection Questions

1. Where have I delayed obedience in something God has clearly shown me to do?

2. How can I strengthen my trust in God so that obedience becomes more natural?

3. What is one practical step of obedience I can take this week—even if it feels costly?

Kingdom Declaration

I walk in obedience.

I will not delay, doubt, or deny what God has spoken.

My "yes" carries weight in the Kingdom.

I choose obedience over popularity.

Obedience over convenience.

Obedience over fear.

I am a Kingdom Carrier—and I obey the voice of the King.

Chapter 7

Carry the Kingdom Until He Comes

"And this gospel of the kingdom will be preached in all the world as a witness to all the nations, and then the end will come."
—Matthew 24:14 (NKJV)

Jesus Is Coming—Not as a Baby, but as a King

The first time He came in a manger.

The next time He's coming with fire in His eyes and a sword in His mouth.

He came once as the Lamb—He's coming again as the Lion.

He came to redeem—He will return to reign.

And until that day—**we carry the Kingdom.**

This is not the hour to relax or retreat.

This is the hour to **rise and run**—to finish the race and carry the fire.

We Are Not Waiting—We Are Working

Some believers act like Jesus' return is a reason to check out, bunker down, and escape.

But Jesus never said, "Sit tight and wait." He said, "Occupy until I come."

We're not just **waiting** for His return—we're **working** while we wait.

Preaching. Praying. Discipling. Serving. Building. Sending.

The gospel of the Kingdom must be preached to all nations—not just to the easy ones.

That's the assignment.

That's the mission.

That's why you're still here.

No Retreat. No Regrets. Just Faithfulness.

When the pressure rises, Kingdom Carriers don't shrink back.

When culture shifts, they don't dilute the truth.

When the world mocks, they stand firm—not out of arrogance, but out of **allegiance** to the King.

We don't carry the Kingdom for applause.

We don't carry it to be liked.

We carry it because it's **life or death**—for nations, neighbourhoods, and next generations.

One day we will stand before Jesus. And on that day, what will matter most is **faithfulness.**

Did we show up?

Did we obey?

Did we love well?

Did we carry the Kingdom?

We Carry with Urgency

This is not a drill.

This is not a dress rehearsal.

Time is short. Eternity is real.

The harvest is ready—and the labourers are few.

But you?

You are an answer to that prayer.

You're not here to survive the times—you're here to serve in them.

To proclaim hope in chaos.

To speak light into darkness.

To carry Jesus into every space He sends you.

The King Entrusted You with His Kingdom

Think about that.

Jesus could have written the gospel in the sky.

He could have sent angels to preach in every city.

But He chose **you.**

He entrusted you with His Spirit, His truth, and His mission.

He put His Kingdom in clay vessels like us—not because we're strong, but because **He is.**

And when we show up with obedience, love, and fire—Heaven backs us up.

He's Coming—So Stay Ready

Jesus warned that many would fall asleep before His return.

But Kingdom Carriers live **awake, alert,** and **active.**

We don't lose heart.

We don't lose focus.

We don't lose time.

We live as those who carry the weight of eternity—because we do.

Every conversation matters.

Every act of obedience matters.

Every moment of surrender matters.

He's coming—and we want to be found **faithful.**

Prayer

Jesus, I believe You are coming again. Help me to live with urgency, purity, and faithfulness. Let me not grow weary or distracted. Fill me with power from on high to carry Your Kingdom until the end. Keep me burning. Keep me surrendered. Keep me watchful. I long to hear "Well done" from Your lips—not because I was perfect, but because I was faithful. Come, Lord Jesus. Until then, I'll carry Your Kingdom. Amen.

Reflection Questions

1. Am I living like someone who truly believes Jesus is returning?

2. Where have I been tempted to slow down, settle, or go silent in my Kingdom calling?

3. What specific ways can I carry the Kingdom more boldly in this season?

Kingdom Declaration

I carry the Kingdom.

I will not grow cold, weary, or distracted.

I live with urgency, purity, and boldness.

I serve the King, and I await His return.

Until He comes—I will pray, preach, and persevere.

Until He comes—I will love, serve, and stand.

Until He comes—I will carry the Kingdom.

Accountability and Covering

"Where there is no counsel, the people fall; but in the multitude of counselors there is safety."

—Proverbs 11:14 (NKJV)

This message is submitted with humility under the counsel and covering of trusted spiritual mentors and Kingdom leaders.

I do not walk alone, nor do I carry this message in isolation.

Kingdom Carriers has been birthed through a life of tested obedience, refined by fire, and supported through the prayers and wisdom of those who know me—and challenge me.

I believe in spiritual authority.

I believe in alignment.

I believe in the safety of accountability.

Too many voices are speaking without covering, and too many gifts are platformed without character. I have no desire to join that crowd.

I am committed to carrying this message with **purity, integrity**, and **fear of the Lord.**

I am not building my brand—I am advancing His Kingdom.

And I'm grateful for the leaders who call me higher, challenge my motives, pray over my life, and help me finish well.

Partner With Us

"How shall they hear without a preacher? And how shall they preach unless they are sent?"

—Romans 10:14–15 (paraphrased)

We exist to carry the Kingdom into **unreached and forgotten places,**

to support the underground church,

and to raise up **labourers for the final harvest.**

This is not a one-man mission.

This is a **Kingdom movement**—and there's room for you.

You can **pray.**

You can **give.**

You can **go.**

You can help us strengthen the Church where it's persecuted and activate the Church where it's passive.

This is not about hype or celebrity. This is about finishing the task.

Jesus said the gospel would be preached to all nations—and then the end would come.

Let's carry the Kingdom—together.

Join the movement.

Website: www.JacobIsaac.co.nz[1]

Email: kinglycomms@gmail.com

1.	http://www.JacobIsaac.co.nz

Other Books by Jacob Isaac

Your Moment to Lead

The first half of *Your Moment to Lead*, focuses on honest and reflective self-assessment, while the second half shows how to move beyond personal limitations creatively.

Your Moment to Lead provides you with the following:

1. Essential leadership skills
2. Self-assessment tools for recognising leadership ability or potential
3. Current research from leading industry publications
4. The importance of character and the role of ethics in leadership
5. Pitfalls to avoid when assuming a leadership role

It's your moment to lead!

Hope Rising

In *Hope Rising*, I examine the subject of hope – what it is and how it's formed. I help you explore why you may have lost hope, and explain how to find it again.

Based on biblical teaching, you will discover:

1. Key factors that influence your levels of hope
2. How your thinking contributes to feelings of hopelessness
3. A greater understanding of how God works and how He will help you
4. How your bad experiences can be used for good
5. How you can become more hopeful, starting now
6. How to plan for a more positive future.

Hope Rising will help you see your life with fresh eyes and lead you into a closer relationship with God.

www.ingramcontent.com/pod-product-compliance
Lightning Source LLC
Chambersburg PA
CBHW030009040426
42337CB00012BA/711